SCRUB
POCKET
DEVOTIONS

A **21-Day Devotional** for
Healthcare Workers

LaShonda Gray, DNP, CRNA

Scrub Pocket Devotions: A 21-Day Devotional for Healthcare Workers
Published by The Open Door Experience LLC
Chicago, Illinois, U.S.A

Gray, LaShonda, Author
SCRUB POCKET DEVOTIONS
LaShonda Gray

First Edition: August 2023
Identifiers: Library of Congress Control Number: 2023912939|
ISBN 978-1-7374669-0-1(paperback) | ISBN 978-1-7374669-2-5 (hardcover) |
ISBN 978-1-7374669-1-8 (eBook)

RELIGION/Christian Living/Devotional
BODY, MIND & SPIRIT/Inspiration & Personal Growth

QUANTITY PURCHASES: Schools, companies, professional groups, clubs, and other organizations may qualify for special terms when ordering bulk quantities of this title. For information, email: hello@theopendoorexperience.com

Contents

Dedication

I dedicate this book to my Lord and Savior, Jesus Christ. I would not be where I am today without His mercy. I credit my success in my career to Him and offer this book as an appreciation of His love and saving grace.

I also dedicate this book to my mother, who saw my potential at a young age and encouraged me to pursue a career in healthcare, which has been one of the best decisions in my life. Her sacrifices and encouragement have played an essential role in my personal growth and in my journey to becoming a certified registered nurse anesthetist (CRNA). I dedicate this book to her with love.

Finally, I acknowledge you, my reader. I dedicate this book to you for your faithfulness to your patients. As a fellow healthcare professional, I realize the commitment that comes with providing excellent patient care, and I see it as a privilege to stand with you in this profession.

Introduction

This devotional can be used by anyone at any stage of life, but it is targeted to those who walk through the doors of a hospital or clinic every day. We are a unique group of people, and it is rare to find Bible-based books that relate to our experiences and the environment in which we work.

As a nurse anesthetist who has been practicing for over twelve years, I understand how busy our schedules can be. We often have only a few moments to pray before we begin or end our shifts.

That's why I've written this book. Each devotional can be read in just a few minutes, so you can quickly get back to caring for your patients.

This devotional is divided into twenty-one days, each day with its own topic or theme. I chose the topics because they are relatable experiences for all healthcare workers.

In the following pages, I pray your heart will be encouraged as you read God's Word and are reminded of how He works through you.

I also hope this devotional finds its way into your *scrub pocket* among all the other important supplies you need every day. Make these devotionals a daily routine over the next twenty-one days (and beyond).

A Note from the Author: Pocket of Wisdom

As a medical professional, you know all too well the convenience of having a pocket on your scrubs. That scrub pocket is one of the most valuable features of your uniform; it carries all the tools and equipment you need to do your job. It's a means to keep items close by and easily accessible, so you don't have to worry about forgetting something important.

Pockets also symbolize preparation. In the parable of the wise and foolish virgins, the wise virgins are prepared for the bridegroom's coming by bringing extra oil for their lamps (Matthew 25:4). In the story of David and Goliath, David uses the stones he placed in his bag to defeat Goliath (1 Samuel 17:40).

Our pockets remind us that we must be prepared for anything. We never know when we'll need something stored in our scrub pockets, just like you never know when you will need God's Word throughout the day.

So put on your scrubs, and let's start this twenty-one-day devotional journey together. We'll explore scripture and discover how to apply these principles to enrich our professional lives today.

LaShonda Gray, DNP. CRNA

Day 1

Divinely Appointed

*Each of you should use whatever gift you
have received to serve others, as faithful
stewards of God's grace in its various forms.*
—1 Peter 4:10 NIV

*I*t wasn't by chance that you were called to healthcare. It may have been through clinical training that you gained the skills required. Or, maybe seeing a family member struggle with their health inspired you to pursue a career in helping others.

In the verse above, we learn that we should serve others as faithful stewards of God's grace in various forms. In a profession as large as the medical field, there are so many ways to make your mark.

Whatever path brought you here, each step was guided by God to get you to this place of service. No other occupation could allow you to make such an impression on someone's life.

Whatever your role—physician, nurse anesthetist, technician, nurse, physical therapist, phlebotomist, dentist, chiropractor, or pharmacist—your daily work is guided by a divine purpose beyond just providing patient care. The gift God has given you helps patients find hope when they feel there is none.

As a believer, you have a unique impact on those you serve. You're not just helping people feel better—you are helping them experience God's healing power! And the best part is that you don't do it alone. You are surrounded by a team of colleagues who share your calling and collaborate with you to meet the diverse needs of every patient.

When you embrace your role in the medical field, you are spreading your light into a dark world and using your God-given talents to help patients overcome sickness and pain.

As you go about the daily grind, do it joyfully, knowing that you are following God's plan for your life by using your gifts and skills to bless all who enter the healthcare system.

There is no greater gift than this!

Prayer

Dear Lord, thank You for the blessed opportunity to practice in this profession. Throughout my day, please help me remember that You are walking beside me each step of the way. Please help me stay mindful of my purpose and serve my patients with their best interests in mind. In Jesus' name, amen.

Additional Scriptures:

Now there are diversities of gifts, but the same Spirit.
(1 Corinthians 12:4)

Having then gifts differing according to the grace that is given to us, whether prophecy, let us prophesy according to the proportion of faith.
(Romans 12:6)

Reflect on how God led you to your career in healthcare. Describe specific examples or times when you felt divine moments led you to this career path.

_____

_____

_____

_____

_____

_____

_____

_____

An Immediate Turnaround

And there came a voice from heaven,
saying, Thou art my beloved Son, in whom
I am well pleased. And immediately the
spirit driveth him into the wilderness.
—Mark 1:11–12

*I*n one significant moment, Jesus came up from the waters of baptism and heard the voice of God affirm that He was pleased him. However, before Jesus could truly enjoy this occasion, the Holy Spirit *immediately* led him into the wilderness for forty days. There, he was tempted by Satan.

Have you ever had days like that? Things are going well, and then suddenly, they're not. You walked into the hospital or clinic feeling confident and ready to care for your patients, but then chaos started unraveling. Or, perhaps, despite your best efforts, your health declines, or your private practice takes an unexpected turn, leaving you wondering about your future.

It's easy to second-guess yourself and wonder why God would allow these things, especially when you've been sowing good seeds.

That is how God works sometimes.

He wants us to experience both sides of the spectrum—the good and bad—to equip us with the resilience to handle any challenge life may present. Most people see the wilderness as a place of tribulation—a place without God, where nothing goes your way, and you continuously suffer. But remember that while you may face troublesome times, moments of joy and restoration will follow.

In fact, in that same chapter, good things happened immediately as well. When Jesus touched Simon's mother-in-law, her fever *immediately* left her (Mark 1:31). Similarly, when Jesus touched the leper, *immediately* the leper was made clean (Mark 1:42). Because of these miracles, Jesus *immediately* became famous throughout the region (Mark 1:28). These verses are a reassuring reminder that good things can happen in the blink of an eye.

On the other side of the wilderness is a season when one good thing happens after another. According to Amos 9:13–15 (MSG), the turnaround will happen so fast that your head will spin in amazement. As a healthcare provider, you know better than anyone else how swiftly things can change.

Embrace the power of timing, because when it's time for you to come out of that wilderness season, an immediate turnaround is not just a maybe or a possibility—it's a promise.

Will you hold on until your season of "*immediately*" comes?

Prayer

Dear Lord, regardless of what the day may bring—whether it is victory or defeat—remind me that You are there with me. May every area of my life be filled with unexpected victories and an abundance of miracles. Extend Your blessings not only to me but to every patient. I speak healing throughout every hospital. Let every infirmity bow at Your name. I pray in faith, knowing You will not withhold any good thing. In Jesus' name, amen.

Additional Scriptures

And suddenly there was a great earthquake, so that the foundations of the prison were shaken: and immediately all the doors were opened, and every one's bands were loosed.
(Acts 16:26)

So Jesus had compassion on them, and touched their eyes: and immediately their eyes received sight, and they followed him.
(Matthew 20:34)

What steps can you take to have faith in God's timing and hold onto the promise that your season of "immediately"—a time of rapid miracles and positive change— could be right around the corner?

Day 3

The Power of Less

*And the Lord said unto Gideon, The people
that are with thee are too many for me
to give the Midianites into their hands,
lest Israel vaunt themselves against me,
saying, Mine own hand hath saved me.*
—Judges 7:2

*Y*ou understand pretty well the challenges of working
in an environment where resources are sometimes limited. Whether you're scrambling to find replacements for
out-of-stock medical supplies or adjusting to staffing shortages, you can quickly feel like the odds are against you.

Gideon probably felt this way, too, as he sought help at a time when there were seemingly not enough people to battle against the Midianites.

But God had other plans.

He told Gideon that his army was too large and that he needed to decrease it significantly. God's instructions may have shocked Gideon, who probably thought that the more soldiers he had, the higher his chances of success.

However, with the Lord's specific directions, Gideon carefully selected only those he believed could conquer the Midianites, slowly decreasing his army until it numbered just three hundred men. Those remaining were not distracted by the small number of soldiers; they were focused entirely on winning the battle.

Often, God does His most remarkable work when you feel you don't have enough. It may not make sense initially, but the message is clear: It's not about what you don't have; size doesn't always guarantee victory. It's about what God can do with what you *do* have.

When you look at how God took Gideon's army of just three hundred men and used them to defeat the thirty-five-thousand-man Midianite army, it should encourage you to keep going forward with whatever little you have.

Remember the story of the fishes and the loaves? When challenged with feeding a huge crowd, the disciples saw how little they had (Matthew 14:17-21). They only had five loaves and two fish—a small amount of food that seemed too little to feed so many people. However, Jesus took what little they had and miraculously fed five thousand people.

This example proves that God doesn't always give you the amount you think you need. Instead, He gives you circumstances that require faith so that you develop the confidence to overcome what appears to be an undefeatable situation.

Push through those times when you feel you don't have enough, and know that God can transform your little into much.

Those times when you feel like you've come up short are often the times when God is getting you ready for a supernatural miracle that only He can bring to pass.

Prayer

Dear Lord, when I feel like I don't have enough and when I feel like my hands are too small to do what needs doing—thank You for showing me Your power. I know that You can turn less into more. Help me trust in Your power, and guide me to provide the best care to those who depend on me. I pray that I will be reminded of Philippians 4:13: "I can do all things through Christ who strengthens me." In Jesus' name, amen.

Additional Scriptures

Then he answered and spake unto me, saying, This is the word of the LORD unto Zerubbabel, saying, Not by might, nor by power, but by my spirit, saith the LORD of hosts.
(Zechariah 4:6)

And Jonathan said to the young man that bare his armour, Come, and let us go over unto the garrison of these uncircumcised: it may be that the Lord will work for us: for there is no restraint to the Lord to save by many or by few.
(1 Samuel 14:6)

Consider the story of Gideon and his army. Reflect on a time in your career when you encountered limited resources. How did you overcome the situation, and what did you learn from it?

Day 4

The Blessing of Forgetting

And Joseph called the name of the firstborn
Manasseh: For God, said he, hath made me
forget all my toil, and all my father's house.
—Genesis 41:51

In the high-stakes environment of healthcare, it may feel impossible to embrace such a concept as forgetting. We remember everything because the repercussions of forgetting something are too great.

Our education and training emphasize the importance of recall—never forgetting a patient's name, allergies, medical histories, or a medication's method of action. Today's scripture, however, offers a different perspective, highlighting the rare instance when forgetting offers relief instead of consequence.

Despite being falsely imprisoned and sold into slavery, Joseph named his firstborn son Manasseh, which means "cause to forget." After Pharaoh promoted Joseph as charge over all of Egypt, Joseph entered a new season of favor, causing him to forget the memories of suffering he faced earlier in life.

We all go through seasons where it feels like "if it isn't one thing, it's another." We're not promised that our lives will be free from trouble, but we are promised that if we hang in there like Joseph, we'll experience blessings again.

A Manasseh season is when you are so blessed that, like Joseph, you forget what once made you fret. It's a season where you *forget* your troubles, and your life becomes so pleasant that the gloomy times in your past are no longer significant.

Forgetting the past does not mean neglecting what you learned during that season. Instead, it means letting go of the hurt it caused you. Isaiah 43:18–19 tells us that when God is doing a new thing, the disappointment of the past has no room to linger.

Despite going through rough times, you have the promise of a Manasseh season. Whether it's an answered prayer in your personal life or a professional goal achieved, one blessing can lead to several more.

Let this scripture inspire you to hold on as you navigate the highs and lows of life beyond the hospital's walls. Remember, a season of Manasseh is on the way, and with it comes a time of positive expectation, a renewed sense of purpose, and the blessing of forgetting.

Prayer

Dear Lord, I am grateful for how You have allowed me to forget my past struggles and move forward, anticipating the good things You have in store for me. I pray for clarity as I go through this chapter of my life. Give me fresh eyes to see what You are doing in this season, and help me give my patients the care they need to heal. In Jesus' name, amen.

Additional Scriptures

Therefore if any man be in Christ, he is a new creature: old things are passed away; behold, all things are become new.
(2 Corinthians 5:17)

Brethren, I count not myself to have apprehended: but this one thing I do, forgetting those things which are behind, and reaching forth unto those things which are before. I press toward the mark for the prize of the high calling of God in Christ Jesus.
(Philippians 3:13–14)

Can you remember a time in your life when a season of blessings came after a difficult time? How did this season impact your professional life?

Day 5

The True Measure of Wealth

For the money faileth.
—Genesis 47:15

We all have our own unique reasons for pursuing careers in healthcare. Many people are drawn to it because it's rewarding. You experience life's beautiful moments, such as the birth of a baby, a successful surgery, or seeing a patient take their first steps after a severe injury. However, this profession is also a constant reminder of how fragile life can be.

So, what happens when the demands of working in healthcare become too much? What do you do when the overtime and extra shifts to make more money begin to take a toll? Many people find motivation in money because it allows them to keep food on the table, go on vacations, and continue pursuing their passion for serving others.

But make no mistake: Money is fleeting. We've all experienced its unpredictable nature in one way or another.

Despite this instability, there's no way to deny the importance of money in our world. We all need it, and let's be honest; most of us want more of it. People often say that you can solve just about any problem if you have enough money. Even Ecclesiastes 10:19 (NIV) says, "Money is the answer for everything."

However, there are situations when money fails us. We pray for solutions, but what we really need may not be found in our bank accounts. Unexpected crises can quickly deplete our resources and leave us financially drained. During these times, we must look beyond our wallets.

Let's look at Mark 5:26, where we see the story of a woman who spent as much as she possibly could to treat her blood issue, but her sickness surprisingly worsened. In this case, even money did not bring healing—only God could do that.

While people may be attracted to the appearance of being well-off, like expensive homes and designer clothes, true wealth is found in knowing that God is our sustainer.

Luke 12:15 (NLT) says, "Life is not measured by how much you own." God has given us so much more than just money—He has given us Himself! That means that through Him, you have access to every single thing you need.

In a world where money is often seen as a prescription to remedy all our troubles, it can be easy to overlook its limits. We must remember that God is our provider. He has the power to raise the dead, as seen in Elijah's prayer in 1 Kings 17, and to increase our resources, as we read in 2 Kings 4. These stories show that God's power and provision exceed even the greatest riches.

With this assurance, when money doesn't quite reach far enough, let us turn to the One who does. He will supply you with what you need when you need it most.

Prayer

Dear Lord, it's tempting to get caught up in working hard to make more money to obtain more things. Help me see that no amount of money can replace what You can do in my life. When I am persuaded to seek security in my possessions, remind me of what is truly important: authentic relationships and Your divine plan for my life. Help me know that even though money may fail me, You never will! In Jesus' name, amen.

Additional Scriptures

*But my God shall supply all your need according
to his riches in glory by Christ Jesus.*
(Philippians 4:19)

*And the Lord shall make thee plenteous in goods,
in the fruit of thy body, and in the fruit of thy cattle,
and in the fruit of thy ground, in the land which
the Lord sware unto thy fathers to give thee.*
(Deuteronomy 28:11)

**How do you find happiness in your
professional life beyond financial gains?**

_____

_____

_____

_____

_____

_____

What Will You Thank God for Today?

*One of them, when he saw he was
healed, came back, praising God in a
loud voice. Jesus asked, "Were not all ten
cleansed? Where are the other nine?"*
—Luke 17:15,17 (NIV)

Every day, we witness miracles: from watching a new born fully recover after months of being in the neonatal intensive care unit (NICU) to the relieving moments when implementing a new skill or procedure comes easily.

We are consistently reminded that God blesses us with more good days than we genuinely appreciate. For instance, maybe you walked into the hospital dreading your

23

assignment or caseload, but it turned out to be a much easier day than you thought.

It can be tempting to forget where these miracles come from—to take them for granted without giving God thanks.

In today's scripture, Jesus speaks of miraculously healing ten lepers. Despite their new well-being, only *one* leper went back and thanked Him. I imagine the other nine were excited about their healing but forgot to appreciate God's hand in their success.

It's not uncommon to fall into that same trap, thinking that all the ways God blesses us are just the norm. When good things happen all the time, it's easy to stop noticing them.

Suppose you stop for a moment and consider all the good things that have happened to you. What about that time you accidentally stuck your finger with a contaminated needle, but your lab results were negative for bloodborne diseases? Or when you forgot to set your alarm clock, but God still woke you up at your normal time so that you were on time for work. It's a miracle that with all the stress in your life, you still passed boards on the first attempt. And let's not forget that colleague who faithfully buys you a coffee when you feel drained.

No matter how often you experience God's favor—no matter how many times He answers your prayers—always be thankful. Not only does it elevate your mood, but more importantly, being thankful aligns you with the will of God, according to 1 Thessalonians 5:18.

Even better, when we're thankful, we invite God to give us more. In 1 Samuel 1, Hannah is a perfect example of this principle. She was barren and prayed so hard for a son. God answered her cry and gave her a son, whom she named Samuel. Hannah praised and *thanked* God for that one son. And then God blessed her even more by giving her *five more* children (1 Samuel 2:21)!

There are so many ways God shows up. You just have to be open to seeing His hand at work. Keep giving God the glory (even for the little things), and be like the one leper who came back to say thank you!

Prayer

Dear Lord, I know there are times when I forget to thank you. Help me remember how blessed I am as You meet my needs every day. Please help me be grateful when You show up unexpectedly, and may I always recognize the blessings that come from serving You. In Jesus' name, amen.

Additional Scriptures

*Enter into his gates with thanksgiving, and into his courts
with praise: be thankful unto him, and bless his name.*
(Psalm 100:4)

*O give thanks unto the Lord; for he is good:
for his mercy endureth for ever.*
(Psalm 136:1)

**Take a moment to list ten ways (both
big and small) God has shown up
for you throughout your workday.
Graciously thank Him for each one.**

_____

_____

_____

_____

_____

_____

Day 7

Is Your Net Working? Or Is It Networking?

And Simon answering said unto him, Master, we have toiled all the night, and have taken nothing: nevertheless at thy word I will let down the net. And when they had this done, they inclosed a great multitude of fishes: and their net brake.
—Luke 5:5–6

Have you ever found yourself repeatedly striving for that promotion or the chance to advance your career, only to feel like it's just out of reach? Maybe you are a medical student determined to match into a residency program or an intensive care nurse with a goal of becoming a certified registered nurse anesthetist. Or, perhaps, you are someone who has been striving to climb the corporate ladder to no avail.

You've put forth your best effort by networking and even taking on extra work to prove yourself. However, you still struggle to get a breakthrough.

In today's scripture, Simon, a skilled fisherman, experiences the same disappointment when he fishes all night and catches nothing. I am sure Simon felt pretty discouraged, thinking he wasted time and energy. However, when Simon follows Jesus' instruction to launch his net again, he catches so many fish that his net breaks! Through Simon's story, we see the advantage of stepping back, having faith, and trying again.

We see a similar instance in the Old Testament (Joshua 6). Think about the Israelites who marched around the Jericho wall seven times before the wall fell flat. Imagine their frustration and doubt as they complete the fifth and sixth laps. The journey took longer than they wanted. Sound familiar? Still, on that seventh lap around, the wall came down!

Sometimes, success is not about networking or who you know—it's about having faith and persistence. There's a popular saying that *insanity* is doing the same thing over and over and expecting different results.

I say that's what *faith* is.

Faith is doing the same thing repeatedly, expecting different results and actually *obtaining* those results. Let this devotional be a reminder that breakthroughs come when we are diligent in our pursuit of them.

Don't be discouraged if your first attempts aren't successful. It's likely that each time you find yourself in a defeating situation, you are actually one step closer to winning. It's not all about networking; it's about trusting in the Lord, who will make your net. . . work.

Launch out again. This time, I believe the net will break in your favor.

Prayer

Dear Lord, bless me with faith to believe everything is possible with You. I am ready to try again, to cast my net into the deep, and to believe that this time I will see the change I seek. I give You all the glory and thank You in advance for what You are about to do in my life. In Jesus' name, amen.

Additional Scriptures

Now pick up the other arrows," said Elisha. He picked them up. Then he said to the king of Israel, "Strike the ground. "The king struck the ground three times and then quit. The Holy Man became angry with him: "Why didn't you hit the ground five or six times? Then you would beat Aram until he was finished. As it is, you'll defeat him three times only."
(2 Kings 13:18–19 MSG)

And he took the blind man by the hand, and led him out of the town; and when he had spit on his eyes, and put his hands upon him, he asked him if he saw ought. And he looked up, and said, I see men as trees, walking. After that he put his hands again upon his eyes, and made him look up: and he was restored, and saw every man clearly.
(Mark 8:23–25)

As you think about your professional goals, reflect on times when you've felt frustrated, similar to Simon. Consider what lessons you can learn regarding relaunching your net and trying again, knowing that God has a unique path for your success.

Day 8

The Value of Mentorship

And Elijah said unto him, Elisha, tarry here, I pray thee; for the Lord hath sent me to Jericho. And he said, As the Lord liveth, and as thy soul liveth, I will not leave thee. So they came to Jericho. . . . And it came to pass, when they were gone over, that Elijah said unto Elisha, Ask what I shall do for thee, before I be taken away from thee. And Elisha said, I pray thee, let a double portion of thy spirit be upon me.
—2 Kings 2:4, 9

Mentorship in healthcare is an inspiring concept, and the story of Elijah and Elisha serves as a perfect example. We see that Elijah was an impactful mentor to Elisha, guiding him and sharing wisdom that would help shape Elisha's future.

Their bond was so strong that Elisha carried on his mentor's legacy even after Elijah's death.

When we think of biblical figures, we often imagine them having a completely unrelatable way of life. The truth is they weren't that different from us. They were everyday people with the same desires as you and me.

This idea of recognizing our own reflection in others helps us understand how mentorship works. When we see someone who looks like us thriving in a field we aspire to pursue, it gives us hope that with hard work and dedication, our own success is attainable.

Many of us look at our colleagues and think they have it all figured out. Despite their confidence, this impression may only sometimes be the case. We all face various challenges, and our peers are no different.

Although Elijah faced moments of despair, he remained an influential mentor whose teachings inspired Elisha to learn from the prophets of God. This experience empowered Elisha to recognize his own abilities as God's servant.

As you progress in your professional life, aim to mirror Elisha's approach: Spend time with mentors, observe their actions, and attentively listen to their counsel. Everything from the standard of patient care to leadership skills can be learned through mentorship.

Also, be willing to share the highs and the lows with your colleagues, remembering that doing so creates a space for everyone to thrive and improve patient care.

Proverbs 15:22 reminds us that seeking advice from others is critical to achieving success. Just as Elisha received a double portion of Elijah's spirit, you, too, can benefit greatly from the wisdom and guidance of those who have gone before you.

Mentorship has been a key aspect of personal development since biblical times. There are countless examples of how God has helped others before you, and rest assured that He will place the right individuals on your path to help you too.

Prayer

Dear Lord, thank you for the benefit of mentorship and the people who have helped me along the way. Please help me be a servant willing to share my knowledge with others so they can grow and thrive clinically. Remind me that my role is not just about teaching someone how to do something but also about providing support as they develop into a competent provider. Thank You for trusting me with this valuable role to improve patient care and to glorify You. In Jesus' name, amen.

Additional Scriptures

Give instruction to a wise man, and he will be yet wiser:
teach a just man, and he will increase in learning.
(Proverbs 9:9)

And Ruth said, Intreat me not to leave thee, or to
return from following after thee: for whither thou
goest, I will go; and where thou lodgest, I will lodge:
thy people shall be my people, and thy God my God.
*(*Ruth 1:16)

Think about a mentor who positively impacted your professional growth. How can you incorporate his or her influential qualities into your future mentorships?

Day 9

Your Miracle Is in What You Hear

So then faith cometh by hearing,
and hearing by the word of God.
—Romans 10:17

Whether it is the sound of a patient's monitor alarming, the beep of a pulse oximeter in the operating room, or the sound of oxygen flowing through a nasal cannula— daily, we hear many sounds reminding us of the importance of our work.

These sounds give us clinical insight into how best to address our patient's needs, but there is a sound more powerful than any of these . . . a sound that breaks down mountains and heals the sick . . . a sound that gives strength to the weary and peace to an anxious heart.

This sound is the Word of God.

What if the miracle you have been asking God for and the answer to your prayer is *not* connected to what you *say* with your mouth but what you *hear* with your ears?

In Matthew 9:27-29, we see two blind men crying out to Jesus to restore their vision. Their miracle manifested not because of what they said with their mouths but due to their faith, which was stirred up by their *hearing*. Hearing Jesus' words gave these men a supernatural healing that would change their lives from that day forward.

We see another example in 1 Kings 18. In verse 1, God tells Elijah that He will send rain upon the earth to end the drought causing the famine. It isn't until verse 41 that Elijah says he *heard* a sound of the abundance of rain. Despite not one raindrop being in sight, Elijah kept the faith in what he *heard*. Sure enough, the sky opened up, fulfilling the Word Elijah *heard* from God. The drought plaguing the earth suddenly ended, confirming that this dry season was over.

When you hear God's Word, unanswered prayer requests lose their power over you. Miracles that have been delayed begin to shift again and take shape. The good seeds you've planted begin to sprout.

Listen closely and take each sound you hear as a reminder to open your heart and mind to the benefit of hearing God's Word. It is through hearing God's Word that our doubts are rendered powerless. Remember, where there is hearing, there is faith, and where there is faith, there are miracles.

Prayer

Dear Lord, I pray that You open my ears to Your Word and that it will manifest in my life. I know Your promises will not be left unfulfilled, so give me strength as I strive each day to hear You. Remove anything hindering my ability to discern Your voice from the many other sounds around me each day, and let the sound of Your Word increase my faith so I may believe again. In Jesus' name, amen.

Additional Scriptures

But he said, Yea rather, blessed are they that hear the word of God, and keep it.
(Luke 11:28)

He that is of God heareth God's words.
(John 8:47)

**How can hearing God's Word
positively influence your perspective,
your clinical decision-making,
and life outside of work?**

_____

_____

_____

_____

_____

_____

_____

_____

Day 10

The One That Can Do Both

Those who were building the wall and those who carried loads did their work with one hand, and held something to fight with in the other hand.
—Nehemiah 4:17

When both of your hands are full, it may seem impossible to balance the demands of work and home life. However, the story of the builders of Jerusalem's wall reminds us that with God's help, we can do both.

Rebuilding the wall of Jerusalem took work, but Nehemiah and his builders were up to the challenge. Unbothered by their adversaries, they balanced

41

reconstructing the wall with one hand while holding their swords in the other to protect themselves from their enemies.

With both of their hands fulfilling tasks, God was with the builders every step of the way, even though opposition stood against them.

Can you see yourself in the same situation as the builders, constantly feeling like both of your hands are overflowing with work and struggling to find a moment to just "be"? Job pressures can easily spill over into your personal life. At the same time, the demands at home can easily interrupt your concentration at work.

Maybe you're a perfusionist managing patients during heart surgery, and you still make time for your son's basketball game after a long and tiring day. Or maybe you are a chiropractor who spends most of the day performing adjustments on patients while also prioritizing your own physical health. Or, perhaps, you are a therapist who listens intently to your client's struggles and is also present for your own family's emotional needs.

Balance plays out differently for everyone, and that's okay. Know that you are fully capable of multitasking. If you think about it, there's nothing that our hands can't accomplish. That's the way God made us.

Your one hand may be dedicated to patient care. At the same time, your other hand holds a long "to-do" list to tackle after work. But remember Nehemiah and the builders whose hands were also accomplishing multiple things but still managed to rebuild a broken wall.

As you walk the hospital's halls, remember that God is with you. Know that He is holding up your hands as you do *His* work—and He is right there with you at home for yours.

Philippians 1:6 says, "he which hath begun a good work in you will perform it until the day of Jesus Christ." One day, just like Nehemiah and the builders, it's possible that you will look back in amazement at the foundations God used your hands to build. Let His arms support you today as you find the perfect balance to continue to do the work He placed before you.

Prayer

Dear Lord, thank You for always being with me wherever I go. I pray that my focus will be renewed so that I may be attentive to the task set before me. Work and life can pull me in different directions, so please give me the strength and ability to do both with ease. In Jesus' name, amen.

Additional Scriptures

Better is an handful with quietness, than both the
hands full with travail and vexation of spirit.
(Ecclesiastes 4:6)

And whatsoever ye do, do it heartily, as
to the Lord, and not unto men.
(Colossians 3:23)

> As you balance the responsibilities in your current practice and your personal life, how can the story of Nehemiah and the builders inspire you? Think about how God's support can enable you to provide quality patient care while being fully present in your personal life.

Day 11

The Pool of Bethesda: A Lesson in Self-Care

*The impotent man answered him, Sir, I have
no man, when the water is troubled, to put
me into the pool: but while I am coming,
another steppeth down before me. Jesus saith
unto him, Rise, take up thy bed, and walk.*
—John 5:7-8

In the Pool of Bethesda story, a disabled man struggles
to get in the pool to experience its healing power. He was
paralyzed and didn't think he could maneuver himself into
the pool. Jesus saw the man's hesitation and encouraged
him to get up and walk. Miraculously, as soon as he did,

after thirty-eight years of suffering, his mobility returned, and he walked!

Whether it's getting adequate sleep or taking a walk to clear your mind, this story is a reminder that it's never too late to prioritize your well-being.

As faithful providers, we can't ignore that we encounter situations that can be emotionally and physically taxing. We're constantly moving from one task to another, and before we realize it, several weeks have gone by without exercise, and we're back to feeling sluggish.

It's easy to think of reasons why you can't pause and "get in the pool." Without knowing it, many of us prioritize our jobs above taking care of ourselves. We often get stuck in the cycle of an everyday routine, making it difficult to take time away from our busy schedules to do something that may seem like a luxury.

While you don't have to go as far as getting in an actual swimming pool, allow yourself time to recharge. Self-care is not just about looking good on the outside—it's also about nurturing your mind. When you make time to reset, you're better prepared to provide high-quality patient care.

The value of self-care is so crucial, whether you are a tech, nurse, physician, or therapist. Involve yourself in the activities that bring you the most joy and make them a regular part of your day.

Self-care might feel like another thing to add to your routine, like washing your hands and staying on top of your charting, but it's much more than that. The goal is to find a way to refresh your mind, body, and soul. Sometimes we need a voice of reassurance, like when Jesus spoke those moving words to the paralyzed man. So don't hesitate: Schedule that time for yourself.

The reward will be worth it.

Prayer

Dear Lord, I seek Your wisdom as I create a schedule for self-care. I pray that You help me order my priorities and arrange my schedule appropriately. Help me find ways to take a step back from my responsibilities and focus on myself, so I can be fully equipped to give excellent care to my patients. In Jesus' name, amen.

Additional Scriptures

*Beloved, I wish above all things that thou mayest
prosper and be in health, even as thy soul prospereth.*
(3 John 1:2)

*For no man ever yet hated his own flesh; but nourisheth
and cherisheth it, even as the Lord the church.*
(Ephesians 5:29)

**List five self-care activities you
will commit to doing today or this
week to show up as your best for
yourself and your patients.**

Day 12

When Change Is Constant

For I am the Lord, I change not.
—Malachi 3:6

Change is an inevitable part of working in healthcare: guidelines change, equipment changes, staffing changes, and even the way you provide care changes. From advancements in medical knowledge to fluctuations in policies, it's impossible to go a day without being impacted by change in some way.

In the midst of all of these variations, remember what the Bible says: God never changes.

We can always lean on Him when things seem unstable. No matter how far healthcare technology advances or how much our understanding of medicine increases, the wisdom within the Bible remains steadfast. The Bible tells us that Jesus Christ is the same yesterday, today, and forever (Hebrews 13:8). When you meditate on God's Word, you get strength from knowing that God does not change! He's always with us in our trials, and His Word keeps us grounded as we encounter unexpected changes.

In the book of Genesis, we read an example of how God used change to bring about His plan. Abraham and Sarah were originally named Abram and Sarai, but God *changed* their names when He revealed they would have a child despite their old age. This was a challenging promise to believe. It meant that Abraham and Sarah had to trust God's change process, even when circumstances seemed doubtful. However, because Abraham and Sarah accepted change, they were blessed with a son who became the ancestor of many nations.

This story proves how God can work through even the most dramatic changes. No matter what changes you encounter in your practice, you can trust that God will bring about something good from it in the end.

As you navigate the dynamics of healthcare, remember that every change has a purpose. It gives us a new perspective that forces us out of our habits and shakes up our routines. The solution to handling change isn't trying to stop it from happening; it's taking each change as a way to trust that all things are working together for your good.

Prayer

Dear Lord, I thank You for being constant. You are consistent even when things around me seem to change at lightning speed. Teach me to view these changes positively, using them as opportunities to grow personally and professionally. In Jesus' name, amen.

Additional Scriptures

The grass withereth, the flower fadeth: but the word of our God shall stand for ever.
(Isaiah 40:8)

God is not a man, that he should lie; neither the son of man, that he should repent: hath he said, and shall he not do it? or hath he spoken, and shall he not make it good?
(Numbers 23:19)

Consider the story of Abraham and Sarah. How can their trust in God's plan for change encourage you to embrace change in your profession?

_____

_____

_____

_____

_____

_____

_____

Day 13

Decisions, Decisions

*Whether you turn to the right or to the
left, your ears will hear a voice behind you,
saying, "This is the way; walk in it."*
—Isaiah 30:21

It's estimated that the average adult makes around thirty-five thousand decisions per day. While this number sounds very high, it's probably not too far off, considering all the choices you must make for yourself, your family, and your patients.

From the minute you wake up in the morning to the time you lay your head down at night, your entire day is spent making decisions. Some of these decisions come naturally—you don't even need to think about them—while others require some pondering.

You are especially prone to making many choices because you have several complex decisions to make regarding your patients each day—if not every minute! The predicament is figuring out how to navigate these critical decisions carefully while keeping everyone's best interests in mind.

Should I observe or admit this patient? Should I give this patient medicine A or medicine B? Should I recommend surgery or physical therapy? Sometimes, there isn't just one correct decision, only varying levels of "right."

The Israelites found themselves in a similar situation. In 1 Kings 18:21, Elijah confronts a group of Israelites and challenges them to decide between two different opinions. They could choose to worship the one and only true God or to worship an idol—Baal.

When Elijah challenged the prophets of Baal to call down fire from heaven, nothing happened. But when Elijah prayed to the God of Israel, the fire of the Lord fell before the people. It was clear to the Israelites whom they should worship.

What do you do when determining the best decision isn't as clear-cut? Do you have a specific process? Do you go with your gut instinct?

When you are stuck between two opinions, remember to trust your expertise and experience, as these are the very reasons you are entrusted with such an important job. Reflect on past clinical scenarios when you made similar decisions, consult with colleagues, and then analyze the outcomes—both the successes and the setbacks. Use all that knowledge to make an intuitive choice that makes you feel good.

Patients are counting on your decision-making skills, and the responsibility to choose can feel heavy. In moments of uncertainty, trust in the Lord, who will guide you through every medical decision giving you a peace only He can bring.

Prayer

Dear Lord, thank You for the guidance You give me every day. I pray that Your Spirit will speak to me clearly, giving me clarity during confusion. May Your wisdom empower me with the discernment I need to accurately assess medical conditions and make appropriate choices for my patients. Please help me know what is right and lead me in the direction You have planned for me and my patients. In Jesus' name, amen.

Additional Scriptures

*I will instruct thee and teach thee in the way which
thou shalt go: I will guide thee with mine eye.*
(Psalm 32:8)

*Trust in the LORD with all thine heart; and lean
not unto thine own understanding. In all thy ways
acknowledge him, and he shall direct thy paths.*
(Proverbs 3:5–6)

**How does your faith in God influence
your decision-making when facing
high-pressure clinical situations?**

Day 14

Shake it Off

*And he shook off the beast into
the fire, and felt no harm.*
—Acts 28:5

The story starts with Paul and other believers sailing to Rome to be tried in court for preaching the gospel.

On their journey, they arrive on an island called Melita. While Paul picks up sticks to start a fire, he is bitten by a beast. Those around him expected him to die immediately, but Paul shook the beast off into the fire and went about his day.

We all have our own beasts we need to shake off—it may be a mentally exhausting shift in the emergency room, a day full of managing multiple consultations, or getting home so late you miss the chance to eat dinner with your family. When the day has been more challenging than we expected, we often let the negativity drag us down into the next day.

We've all been there.

But if you have ever experienced pain, you know it does not hurt forever. Without knowing it, we often become weighed down by our hard days, carrying them like heavy burdens into the next. But instead of letting the very thing intended to bring you down stay attached to you, do like Paul and shake it off.

What's important is that you learn from yesterday and do better today. Remember that with God on your side, you can overcome anything that seems impossible.

When you wake up in the morning, don't start your day with the negativity of the day before. Each day offers a fresh start. Every morning, you get to switch things up, to manage your patients differently, and to think differently.

Shaking off the beast of yesterday is a choice you must make every morning when you get out of bed, and your feet hit the floor. Be determined to release yourself from the past and step forward with a new mindset. As you do this, remember what God says in Isaiah 45:2 (NIV); He says, "I will go before you. . .and will level the mountains." He is already clearing your path, putting things in place, and paving the way for a better day.

As you walk into your patient's room today, shake off whatever happened yesterday. Put away any lingering frustrations and start over as you approach each patient with skill and a clean slate.

When you do that, you free yourself to completely engage with your patients and accomplish whatever comes your way.

Prayer

Dear Lord, please give me the strength to let go of yesterday's burdens. Allow me to begin again and focus on the care of my patients. Help me shake off the bad days and focus on how You brought me through. Let me realize that although I may face trials, there is fullness of joy in Your presence. Thank You for restoring my spirit and watching over me. In Jesus' name, amen.

Additional Scriptures

*Behold, I give unto you power to tread on serpents
and scorpions, and over all the power of the enemy:
and nothing shall by any means hurt you.*
(Luke 10:19)

*And the LORD sent fiery serpents among the people, and
they bit the people; and much people of Israel died. And
Moses made a serpent of brass, and put it upon a pole,
and it came to pass, that if a serpent had bitten any
man, when he beheld the serpent of brass, he lived.*
(Numbers 21:6, 9)

**What strategies can you put into practice to
shake off yesterday and start each day with a
fresh outlook to better serve your patients?**

Day 15

In the Beginning

Do not despise these small beginnings, for
the Lord rejoices to see the work begin.
—Zechariah 4:10 (NLT)

We all start as beginners at some point in our careers. Even experienced nurses, surgeons, and technicians still learn new skills—learning is ongoing.

When the day comes to start something new, you may look at the task with uncertainty. A new beginning often comes with many questions: Will I perform well? Will my patients benefit from my performance? Will I overcome the steep learning curve? What if I fail?

You could be a new nurse starting your first day on the job, a surgeon learning a new procedure, or a dentist developing a unique treatment plan for a patient.

Feeling like a novice again can be uncomfortable because we want to master things quickly, but getting good at something takes time and practice. When God created the world (Genesis 1:1), the Earth was initially nothing. It was through a day-by-day process that God created the world in which we now live.

When God speaks in Zechariah 4:10, He reminds you that even though you may not feel confident at the beginning, He rejoices in your progress—even if it is small.

He will encourage you as you continue to work toward your goal, no matter how far away it may feel.

The similarities between Genesis 1:1 and working in healthcare show us that starting something new may take time to produce the expected outcome. But with time and patience, you will begin to see the shift from novice to expert. As each day goes by, you become more knowledgeable and skilled.

Regardless of the type of beginning, the message is still the same: God knows our beginnings are important, and it's okay if they're a little bumpy. Embrace the bumps. It's good to remember our beginnings; they remind us that nothing improves on its own. Every perfected end starts with a beginning that requires effort, practice, and time.

No matter how small it may be, your beginning deserves a celebration.

Prayer

Dear Lord, You have blessed me with the opportunity for a new beginning. As I begin this new season of my professional life, I pray that You will watch over me. Help me be confident in myself and the clinical skills You have given me. Remind me that You are always with me and encouraging me from start to finish. Let Your angels stay encamped around me as I joyfully embrace new beginnings. In Jesus' name, amen.

Additional Scriptures

Though thy beginning was small, yet thy latter end should greatly increase.
(Job 8:7)

It is like a grain of mustard seed, which a man took, and cast into his garden; and it grew, and waxed a great tree; and the fowls of the air lodged in the branches of it.
(Luke 13:19)

Consider the importance of embracing and celebrating small victories in your daily practice. How do you believe celebrating small successes and beginning something new can improve patient care?

Day 16

Follow the Cloud

And the Lord went before them by day in
a pillar of a cloud, to lead them the way.
—Exodus 13:21

You've heard the term "black cloud," right? Often, you'll hear those words in reference to a coworker who has unusual or unfortunate circumstances occur to them. Maybe you have a colleague who consistently draws the short straw, gets the worst call shifts, or seems to attract clinical disasters like a magnet. They are the ones where the black cloud literally follows them everywhere, to the point where you do your best to avoid working with or near them, fearing that this "black cloud" could rub off on you. We all know this colleague.

65

Or maybe it's you.

Let's take a page from the children of Israel's story as they journeyed from Egypt. They were chased by Pharaoh's army, with the Red Sea in front of them, and led into the wilderness, where they felt like they were going to die. This definitely sounds like a black cloud experience to me.

However, we read in Exodus 13:21 that the Lord went before them in a pillar of a cloud to lead the way. The cloud was for guidance, not a means to keep sending bad situations their way. God never left them; He revealed himself before them by sending a pillar of fire and smoke. He became their "black cloud." Even when they faced the Red Sea, God parted it so they could walk across on dry ground (Exodus 14), and when they met their enemies, He gave them victory over them (Exodus 17).

Stepping back, what if we changed our viewpoint on the black cloud?

Think about it. How often have you encountered a challenging clinical scenario, only to come out of that experience with a deeper understanding? Maybe it was a patient with a rare medical problem, or a complex surgical case that pushed you passed your limits.

When challenging situations happen during your workday, see it as God guiding you rather than disasters following you. The moments that test us the most are often the ones that help shape us into better providers.

God doesn't want you to rely on your own understanding or rush to conclusions based on your limited ability to see His divine plan. He wants you to look up and acknowledge His presence. He is there walking before you as you enter your patient's room. He is already several steps ahead of you, leading you through every clinical scenario and all the long shifts.

You may not understand why unfortunate situations happen, but one thing is for sure: God does. Just as God's presence was with the children of Israel as they went through the desert, He is with you while you go through dark times—even if it's just a tough day at work.

This black cloud could just be a passing storm.

Keep moving forward.

Prayer

Dear Lord, I pray that my black cloud will become a silver lining. When things seem dark, please let me know You are still there. I pray that when I encounter obstacles, I see them as something to overcome rather than something to frustrate me. Anoint my hands with healing and let every step I take be toward a successful outcome. In Jesus' name, amen.

Additional Scriptures

Moreover, brethren, I would not that ye should be ignorant, how that all our fathers were under the cloud, and all passed through the sea; And were all baptized unto Moses in the cloud and in the sea.
(1 Corinthians 10:1–2)

He spake unto them in the cloudy pillar: they kept his testimonies, and the ordinance that he gave them.
(Psalm 99:7)

Consider how you can reframe your "black cloud" experiences in your current practice as a means for professional growth and spiritual development.

_____

_____

_____

_____

_____

_____

Day 17

Remember His Word

*In the multitude of my thoughts within
me thy comforts delight my soul.*
—Psalm 94:19

Do you ever finish your workday only to be bombarded by endless questions, making it hard to truly disconnect? Did I remember to sign that order? Did I remember to take the tourniquet off of the patient's arm? Did I remember to call back the person who paged me?

Your mind is constantly filled with multiple thoughts. You think about the patients you just saw, those you will see tomorrow, and those you handed off to another provider.

Fortunately, you've been trained to juggle multiple thoughts, and it shows in how well you multitask as you practice. However, those very thoughts can also keep you up at night or distract you while in line at the grocery store if you don't take a moment to unplug.

The world can be a loud place full of distractions. If you focus totally on the thoughts that worry you, you may lose sight of what brings you peace. There will always be thoughts and concerns, but remember that God's Word is an anchor through it all.

Let today's verse be a reminder to not only focus on treating your patients and recalling all the important things throughout your day but also remember the one thing that brings inner stillness.

That comfort is found in God's Word.

Whether you read a Bible verse before work in the morning or listen to a sermon as you drive home from work, incorporate a way to add God's Word to your daily thoughts.

Finding peace in God's Word does not mean ignoring your responsibilities; it means renewing your mind with the word of God so that you can face your day with a clear mind.

When you intentionally disconnect from your day and remember God's Word, you then find a way to settle your thoughts.

God gave us His Word to comfort us when our minds are tempted with anxious thoughts. Remember, in Philippians 4:8, Paul tells us to think about whatever is just, pure, and of good report—a verse that reminds us of God's reassuring Word, even when our thoughts are many.

Take a moment now and quiet your mind.

Prayer

Dear Lord, thank You for Your Word and the peace it brings me. Thank You for the blessing of a quiet place to settle down when my mind feels overwhelmed. Help me remain mindful of the things I do during my day so I stay balanced in body and spirit. Give me the privilege to see Your hand at work, and may it bring healing to every patient I meet. In Jesus' name, amen.

Additional Scriptures

As one whom his mother comforteth, so will I comfort you; and ye shall be comforted in Jerusalem.
(Isaiah 66:13)

From the end of the earth will I cry unto thee, when my heart is overwhelmed: lead me to the rock that is higher than I.
(Psalm 61:2)

Which Bible verses bring you comfort when you feel overwhelmed?

Day 18

The 5:00 a.m. Feeling

*This is the day which the Lord hath
made, we will rejoice and be glad in it.*
—Psalm 118:24

It's 5:00 a.m., and you're struggling to get out of bed. You think about your day and the "I don't know if I can do this today" feeling comes over you.

Maybe you're a nurse who manages critical patients or a phlebotomist unable to calm an anxious patient afraid of needles. Or, you're a paramedic tending to multiple traumas on your shift. Some days, the thought of another round of patients feels like too much.

Even though this feeling is often temporary, it can really put a damper on your day if you let it remain.

Although our work could *never* compare to the work of Jesus Christ, even Jesus had a day when He did not want to fulfill the work He was called to do. In Luke 22, we see Jesus praying and asking his Father if there was another way to accomplish the work He was sent to do. The scripture says Jesus was so distressed that His sweat fell like great drops of blood. Can you imagine being this stressed out about your workday? Even still, Jesus chose to keep going and fulfill His mission.

Rest assured; you don't have to wake up feeling happy and upbeat every day. It's okay if you don't feel 100 percent motivated. Today's scripture reminds us that if we're willing to declare the kind of day we want to have early on, we set the tone for the rest of the day.

Today is an entirely blank canvas without any mistakes; it's unblemished by your thoughts and assumptions. When you wake up in the morning—before you've had your coffee or brushed your teeth—think about what the day has to offer.

Picture yourself having an easy day. See yourself overcoming difficulties to provide the best care to your patients. You may not feel like it when your alarm goes off, but in this moment, you're being asked to make a choice. You can let your day happen to you, or you can declare what kind of day you want to have.

Either way, you don't have to wait and see how your day goes before you feel joy or happiness—you can choose them.

You only have today once, so why not declare it a joyous one?

Prayer

Dear Lord, thank You for waking me up this morning and inviting me to make it a great day. As I look forward to this day, help me remember that if I decree a thing, it shall be established (Job 22:28). Guide my decisions with every patient, and may this day be filled with enjoyment and all the things that make me smile from the inside out. In Jesus' name, amen.

Additional Scriptures

Rejoice evermore.
(1 Thessalonians 5:16)

Sing, O daughter of Zion; shout, O Israel; be glad and rejoice with all the heart, O daughter of Jerusalem.
(Zephaniah 3:14)

Consider your morning routine.
What declarations or affirmations
can you incorporate to help you
experience the kind of day you want
to see, according to Psalm 118:24?

Day 19

The One Thing You Must Do Today

And Jesus answered and said unto her,
Martha, Martha, thou art careful and troubled
about many things: But one thing is needful:
and Mary hath chosen that good part,
which shall not be taken away from her.
—Luke 10:41–42

Do you ever feel like Martha—overwhelmed by the endless tasks that come your way each day? You stay up late studying new treatments and attend multiple conferences each year to stay current on the latest medical advancements. Still, each day comes with new clinical scenarios and challenges to overcome.

Even in these moments, Jesus says, "One thing is needful."

Your calling is not to get flustered about the problems you see every day; it is to trust God with them.

In this scripture, Mary didn't turn away from the negative. She decided that the good things were more important. Mary is an excellent example of how to live out your purpose. When she had an opportunity to be with Jesus, she didn't say no—she made time for it. She approached her day with wisdom, recognizing that this one thing was greater than her worries and concerns.

When you feel overwhelmed by the demands of your role, remember Mary's mindset: one of prioritizing quality time with the Lord.

It's easy to fixate on the complexities of your day. The goal is to be like Mary and see the good in it. Think about the patients you've helped, the families that appreciate you, and the colleagues you've collaborated with to provide the best patient care.

And the best part? This good part cannot be taken away from you. Why? Because it's not something superficial. It's something that happens on the inside of you that no one can ever take from you.

Whether you praise yourself for making it through another tiring call shift or take a break from rounding on patients to read a Bible verse, release your worries, and make room for things that truly matter.

Whatever it might be, choose the good part.

Prayer

Dear Lord, help me to prioritize spending time with You so that I may be uplifted and encouraged. As I take care of patients each day, please help me remember and appreciate the moments of happiness and pleasure that come from providing care. Give me peace as I commit myself daily to extending Your healing power. In Jesus' name, amen.

Additional Scriptures

Come unto me, all ye that labour and are heavy laden, and I will give you rest. Take my yoke upon you, and learn of me; for I am meek and lowly in heart: and ye shall find rest unto your souls. For my yoke is easy, and my burden is light.
(Matthew 11:28–30)

"Thy word is a lamp unto my feet,
and a light unto my path."
(Psalm 119:105)

Write down any concerns, and then release them to God.

_____

_____

_____

_____

_____

_____

Day 20

When Iron Swims: Regaining Your Motivation

*But as one was felling a beam, the axe
head fell into the water: and he cried, and
said, Alas, master! for it was borrowed. And
the man of God said, Where fell it? And he
shewed him the place. And he cut down a
stick, and cast it in thither; and the iron did
swim. Therefore said he, Take it up to thee.
And he put out his hand, and took it.*
—2 Kings 6:5–7

Have you ever felt burned out? Have you ever felt like
today looks like yesterday, and tomorrow will likely

look like today? You can't pinpoint exactly when you lost your motivation; you just know that at some point, it got harder to get up in the morning.

The servant in this passage of scripture was working hard to cut down trees with his axe, and then at some point, the axe's head fell off into the water.

There may be times when you feel like the heavy iron axe head mentioned in today's scripture as your motivation to keep going begins to sink. We all know that iron is very heavy, but despite this, the scripture says the iron axe head not only floated to the surface of the water but even started swimming so that Elisha could grab it!

When was the last time you saw iron swim?

This is an example of the power of faith—when you have faith, even the heaviest situations you encounter become light. When the axe head fell into the river, it wasn't lost for good. Elisha's faith in God caused him to get it back.

You may not relate to having an axe head fall into the water, but you can relate to losing motivation. Once you identify how and why you lost your motivation, take steps to get it back.

For the prophet, he tossed a stick in the water. For you, it may be changing how you approach your workday, setting new career goals, or simply asking God to restore you.

Take, for instance, the story of Elijah in 1 Kings 19, who was depressed after receiving threats from Jezebel. Even though Elijah had done some good things in his life, he felt like he could not go any further. His sadness was so intense that he pleaded with God to end his life. Then something miraculous happened—the angel of the Lord touched him and told him to eat to regain his strength. It seems simple, right? But that simple action motivated Elijah to keep pushing forward and continue his mission.

Another example is David, whose motivation came from remembering how God had rescued him from a bear and a lion. So, when he faced Goliath, he knew he could trust God to see him through again (1 Samuel 17:37).

All these individuals were successful because, one way or the other, they regained their motivation.

If God could bring an iron axe head back up from beneath the water so the servant could continue his work, then surely, He can provide you with the motivation needed to stay afloat in this field.

What's important to know is that motivation can be found in the simplest, most unexpected places. The key is to find something that moves you to keep going. When you find it, hold on to it with both hands, and don't let it go.

Prayer

Dear Lord, I pray that Your Spirit reignites my motivation to continue practicing in healthcare, allowing me to defeat burnout. Please give me a steadfast spirit that never wavers. And help me to remain in joy as I fulfill my calling. In Jesus' name, amen.

Additional Scriptures

Therefore, my beloved brethren, be ye stedfast, unmoveable, always abounding in the work of the Lord, forasmuch as ye know that your labour is not in vain in the Lord.
(1 Corinthians 15:58)

And the Lord said unto Moses, Put forth thine hand, and take it by the tail. And he put forth his hand, and caught it, and it became a rod in his hand.
(Exodus 4:4)

What strategies will you implement to prevent burnout? How can you incorporate your faith into these strategies to remain motivated in your current practice?

_____

_____

_____

_____

_____

_____

_____

_____

Day 21

A Dose of Determination

But Moses' hands were heavy; and they
took a stone, and put it under him, and he
sat thereon; and Aaron and Hur stayed up
his hands, the one on the one side, and the
other on the other side; and his hands were
steady until the going down of the sun.
—Exodus 17:12

Moses went to the top of the hill with the rod of God in hand to help the children of Israel win the battle against the Amalekites. Despite his fatigue, with Aaron and Hur holding up his hands, Moses endured all day and night.

The children of Israel may not have seen the heaviness Moses went through to keep them winning, but they saw the outcome of his efforts. Moses' perseverance made a significant difference in a battle that could have ended very differently. The same rod that was used to bring water from a rock (Numbers 20:11) and parted the Red Sea (Exodus 14:16) was the same rod Moses held in his hand to help Israel prevail in battle. His determination paid off.

This is why we should appreciate the power of being determined to show up.

Have you ever had to stay determined even when others didn't notice your efforts?

Your patients and colleagues may never know the struggles you face behind the scenes. Your patients didn't know you were up all night with your sick child or the sad news you received about a family member, but you still showed up to work the next day. Your colleagues didn't know that your car broke down, but you called a neighbor for a ride to make sure you were on time to take report from the previous shift. No one knew about the tears you cried while you drove to work after a breakup with your significant other or the last-minute arrangements you made when the electricity went out in your home.

Some people may say these things are just a part of life. And they are. But wouldn't it be nice to be rewarded for showing up on days like this when you could have easily taken the day off?

Your patients and coworkers only see the end result; they just know that you showed up to work. They don't really feel the fight it took and the hurdles you jumped over to get there. But, despite obstacles, you put on your scrubs each day and show up for your patients and colleagues. Know that God notices your faithfulness. He sees your determination, even when no one else does.

The truth is, you needed to be at work to comfort that patient before their procedure and to catch that near-miss error. It had to be you. It could have gone another way, but your presence ensured it was a victory.

Even when Moses wanted to give up because circumstances seemed too great, God asked Moses in Exodus 4:2, "What is that in thine hand?" That rod in Moses' hand turned what appeared to be a grim situation into a miracle, not once but many times.

And that is my question to you. What is that in your hand? If it's just a tiny bit of determination or faith as small as a mustard seed, take that with you.

And as you continue to give your all to your patients, remember that Matthew 6:4 says that the Lord sees what you do in secret, and He will reward you openly.

Stay determined. We need you.

Prayer

Dear Lord, I thank You for continuing to work through me as I make a difference for each patient I encounter. I ask that You anoint me with determination and instill in me the knowledge that my labor is not in vain. I pray that my career be a testimony to every person I meet. Continue to guide me on this journey, and may all I do bring honor to You. In Jesus' name, amen.

Additional Scriptures

Wherefore lift up the hands which hang down, and the feeble knees.
(Hebrews 12:12)

And let us not be weary in well doing: for in due season we shall reap, if we faint not.
(Galatians 6:9)

Reflect on the perseverance of Moses
as he helped the children of Israel in
various ways. Recall a time when your
determination positively impacted
the life of one of your patients.

Conclusion

As the author of this twenty-one-day daily devotional, I am grateful for your dedication and service. I hope this book has been a source of strength, inspiration, and spiritual rejuvenation for you. Remember, God is always with you, guiding your hands to make a positive difference in the lives of your patients. May you continue to find faith, peace, and joy in your work, and may God bless you abundantly in all you do.

About the Author

Dr. LaShonda Gray has fulfilled various roles in the health-care industry, with a career spanning over two decades. Growing up in the Midwest, Dr. Gray attended the University of Pittsburgh for her Master's and Doctoral Degrees in Nurse Anesthesia. As a certified registered nurse anesthetist (CRNA), she understands the benefits of balancing work and spending quality time with God.

With a desire to uplift her colleagues, Dr. Gray created her debut book, *Scrub Pocket Devotions*. This innovative resource offers meaningful reflections and prayers to help healthcare professionals stay grounded in their faith and find renewed strength for the days ahead.

Made in the USA
Columbia, SC
13 December 2023

28427270R00064